HOUSE OF ABUNDANCE PUBLICATIONS

The Abyss Above

Mind-Blowing Facts About Astronomy, the Cosmos, and Outer Space

Exploration is in our nature. We began as wanderers, and we are wanderers still. We have lingered long enough on the shores of the cosmic ocean. We are ready at last to set sail for the stars

CARL SAGAN

Contents

1 Introduction   1

2 What is Astrology?   3

3 Galaxies - Vast Cosmic Islands   8

4 Exploring the Universe - From Dwarfs to Supergiants   15

5 Dark Matter and Cosmic Mysteries   20

6 Astounding Phenomena in Space   24

7 Unveiling the Local Group: A Galactic Ensemble of Marvels...   27

8 Cosmology - The Study of the Universe   32

9 Astronomy vs. Astrophysics   37

10 Amateur Astronomy - Unveiling the Transient   42

11 Conclusion   47

Epilogue   50

Charting the Course: Help Us with Your Review   53

Resources   54

1

Introduction

I magine gazing at a midnight sky, where the cosmos unfolds before your eyes like a celestial tapestry. Each twinkling star, every mysterious planet, and the vastness of space itself hold secrets waiting to be revealed. Welcome to "The Abyss Above: Mind-Blowing Facts About Astronomy, the Cosmos and Outer Space," an awe-inspiring journey through the wonders of astronomy.

Have you ever wondered what lies beyond our blue planet? Are you curious about the enigmatic forces that shape galaxies or the mind-boggling phenomena that occur millions of light-years away? If so, prepare to embark on an extraordinary quest for knowledge.

In this captivating book, we'll embark on an interstellar expedition, delving into the depths of space and time. We'll unveil the mind-bending facts that will make you question the very fabric of our universe. Every chapter will reveal astonishing revelations, from the birth of stars in colossal nebulae to the earth-shattering death of massive supernovae.

But this journey isn't just about scientific discoveries. It's about the stories woven into the cosmos. We'll reveal the ancient tales of constellations that have captivated humanity for centuries. We'll explore the myths and legends that bridge the gap between science and imagination, reminding us that the beauty of the cosmos is as much about wonder as it is about knowledge.

As we explore the grandeur of black holes, where gravity bends time and space. Witness the intricate dance of planetary systems, where the possibility of extraterrestrial life looms tantalizingly close. Marvel at the cosmic ballet of galaxies colliding, giving birth to new stars, and reshaping the very face of the universe.

"The Abyss Above" will ignite your passion for the cosmos through vivid storytelling and expert insights. Whether you're an aspiring astronomer or simply an admirer of the night sky, prepare to be captivated by the wonders that await.

So, fasten your cosmic seatbelt, for the journey into the infinite expanse of the universe is about to begin. Get ready to embark on an adventure that will expand your mind and leave you in awe of the vast, magnificent celestial mosaic we call the cosmos.

2

What is Astrology?

Definition and Exploration of Astronomy As a Natural Science

Astronomy, a natural science, involves the study of celestial objects and phenomena in the vast universe. Astronomers seek to understand the stars, planets, galaxies, and other cosmic entities through scientific methods and tools. This observational science utilizes telescopes, satellites, and advanced instruments to collect data of the cosmos.

Astronomy primarily aims to trace the origins and evolution of celestial bodies and the universe itself. By analyzing the light emitted or reflected by distant objects and observing changes in their properties and positions, astronomers clarify the cosmic timeline and gain insights into the universe's early stages.

Astronomy also contributes to understanding the physical laws governing the cosmos. By studying the behavior of astral bodies, astronomers test and refine theories related to gravity, electromagnetism, and nuclear physics. Collaborating with physics, chemistry, and planetary science experts, astronomers explore the connections between planetary systems and the underlying physical and chemical processes.

As we explore astronomy as a natural science, we embark on a journey that reveals the wonders of the cosmos. From uncovering the complexities of distant galaxies to studying the planetary dynamics within our solar system, astronomers push the boundaries of knowledge and expand our cosmic horizons. Through their efforts, we gain a deeper appreciation for the immense beauty, diversity, and grandeur of the universe we call home.

The Distinction Between Astronomy and Astrology

As we dive deeper into the captivating realm of astronomy, it is crucial to clarify a common misconception: the distinction between astronomy and astrology. While both fields share a historical connection, they have evolved into distinct disciplines with different aims and methodologies.

As we have learned, astronomy is a scientific endeavor focused on studying cosmic entities. It seeks to understand the laws and mechanisms that govern the universe through empirical observation, mathematical models, and rigorous experimentation. Astronomy explores the physical properties, behaviors, and interactions of celestial bodies, shedding light on the nature of the cosmos.

On the other hand, astrology is a belief system that posits a connection between astronomical bodies and human affairs. It claims that the positions and movements of celestial bodies, particularly the Sun, Moon, planets, and constellations, can influence and provide insights into human personalities, relationships, and even future events. Astrology often involves horoscopes, zodiac signs, and interpretations based on supposed astrological influences.

While astronomy relies on the scientific method, evidence-based research, and objective analysis, astrology is rooted in subjective interpretations and personal beliefs. The methods employed in astrology lack scientific rigor and are not subjected to empirical testing. Therefore, astrology does not adhere to the rigorous standards of evidence and verification upheld by astronomy.

It is crucial to differentiate between these two disciplines to avoid confusion and maintain the integrity of scientific inquiry. Astronomy delves into the vast cosmic wonders to understand the universe's mechanics. At the same time, astrology offers a belief system centered on the perceived influence of celestial objects on human lives.

In the following chapters of this book, we will continue to explore the captivating realms of astronomy, unveiling incredible facts about the cosmos, its celestial inhabitants, and the remarkable forces that shape our universe. Together, let us journey further into the depths of knowledge and wonder as we embrace the scientific marvels of astronomy and leave behind the realms of astrology.

Historical Significance of Astronomy in Different Cultures

Throughout the ages, astronomy has held immense significance in various cultures worldwide. From the earliest civilizations to today, humanity's fascination with the night sky has shaped our understanding of the cosmos and influenced cultural beliefs, rituals, and scientific advancements.

For instance, the ancient Egyptians developed a sophisticated astronomy system tied to their religious practices. They observed the movements of celestial bodies, such as the Sun, Moon, and stars, to develop calendars and align their religious ceremonies with astronomical events. The pyramids were designed with celestial alignment, showcasing the deep intertwining of astronomy and Egyptian culture.

Babylonians, renowned for their astronomical achievements, meticulously recorded celestial observations on clay tablets. They established a calendar based on lunar phases and developed mathematical methods to predict celestial events. Their knowledge of celestial motions laid the foundation for later astronomical advancements in Mesopotamia and beyond.

Ancient Greek civilization birthed notable astronomers like Aristotle, Hipparchus, and Ptolemy, who sought to explain the movements of celestial bodies and develop cosmological models. Greek philosophers pondered the nature of the universe and its place in the grand scheme of existence, leaving an indelible mark on the history of astronomy.

In India, ancient astronomers made significant contributions to astronomy and mathematics. The concept of zero, essential to modern numerical systems, originated in Indian mathematical texts. Astronomical observations in India were essential for religious and agricultural purposes and the development of precise calendars.

The Chinese civilization cultivated a rich astronomical tradition, observing and recording celestial events for centuries. They carefully documented supernovae, comets, and solar eclipses, attributing cultural and political significance to these celestial features. Chinese astronomers also developed accurate astronomical instruments and mathematical models, contributing to understanding celestial motions.

Indigenous peoples of the Americas, such as the Maya and various Native American tribes, possessed meticulous astronomical knowledge. They built elaborate observatories and monuments aligned with celestial events, reflecting their deep spiritual connection to the cosmos and their reverence for celestial bodies.

These examples merely scratch the surface of the diverse cultural significance of astronomy throughout history. It highlights the universal human curiosity about the stars and the profound impact celestial observations have had on societies across the globe.

In the following chapters of this book, we will continue exploring astronomy's wonders, building upon the rich historical legacy left by these cultures. We will uncover more incredible facts about the cosmos, expanding our understanding of the universe's intricacies and our place within it.

3

Galaxies - Vast Cosmic Islands

Definition and Components of Galaxies

Step into the captivating realm of galaxies, the majestic cosmic constellations scattered throughout the vast expanse of the universe. Within this chapter, we embark on a journey to comprehend the essence of galaxies and immerse ourselves in their enchanting components, unveiling the mysteries and marvels that lie within these celestial wonders.

Galaxies are vast systems of stars, stellar remnants, interstellar gas, dust, and dark matter, all intricately bound together by the force of gravity. These cosmic entities serve as the universe's building blocks, each with its unique structure, properties, and cosmic story.

Within galaxies, stars shine as celestial beacons, illuminating the darkness of space. These stars vary in size, mass, and temperature, forming the mesmerizing mosaic that adorns the galaxies we observe. Galaxies are embellished with a kaleidoscope of solar wonders, from newborn stars nestled within stellar nurseries to ancient giants that have burned bright for eons.

Stellar remnants, such as white dwarfs, neutron stars, and black holes, further enrich the fancy stellar networks of galaxies. These lingering remnants stand as testaments to the celestial bodies that have concluded their life cycles, leaving behind traces of their once-majestic existence. They hold the key to understanding the dramatic processes that occur within galaxies, from stellar birth to explosive deaths.

Interstellar gas and dust pervade galaxies, creating the cosmic nurseries where new stars are born. These molecular clouds and nebulae provide the raw materials for forming stars and planetary systems. They shimmer with vibrant colors and intricate structures, showcasing the dynamic interplay between gravity, radiation, and interstellar matter.

Dark matter, a mysterious substance that eludes direct detection, plays a significant role in the dynamics of galaxies. Its gravitational influence shapes the structure and behavior of galaxies, holding them together and driving their elaborate dance across the cosmic stage. Dark matter remains a question, yet its presence serves as a reminder of the hidden depths that pervade the cosmos.

As we explore the components of galaxies, we embark on a journey through the intricate web of stellar systems that populate the universe. Together, we will uncover the mind-boggling diversity, immense scales, and awe-inspiring beauty that galaxies possess. So, brace yourself as we venture further into the heart of these cosmic islands, unlocking the secrets they hold and expanding our understanding of the cosmos.

Overview of the Milky Way Galaxy and its Significance

Amidst the vast array of galaxies scattered throughout the cosmos, there is one that holds exceptional importance for us: the Milky Way. Within this segment, we embark on a captivating odyssey through our very own galactic abode, revealing its mesmerizing characteristics and delving into its profound relationship with our existence.

The Milky Way is a barred spiral galaxy characterized by its distinct spiral arms that wrap around a central bar-shaped structure. Our Solar System, with its planets, moons, and countless other celestial objects, resides within the expansive boundaries of this remarkable cosmic entity.

Stretching across a staggering diameter of at least 26,800 parsecs (87,400 light-years), the Milky Way boasts a dazzling array of celestial wonders. Its spiral arms house vast collections of stars, interstellar gas, and dust, creating regions of intense stellar formation and cosmic beauty. Stellar clusters, nebulae, and stellar nurseries within the Milky Way serve as celestial cradles for the birth and evolution of new stars.

At the heart of the Milky Way lies a supermassive black hole known as Sagittarius A-star. With a mass equivalent to four million times that of our Sun, this gravitational massive entity influences the surrounding stars, contributing to our astrophysical home's compounded dynamics and structure.

The Milky Way's significance to humanity extends beyond its physical attributes. Throughout history, cultures across the globe have gazed up at the night sky, marveling at the band of diffuse light that spans across the heavens. This ethereal band, known as the Milky Way, has inspired myths, legends, and artistic expressions, connecting humanity to the vastness of the cosmos.

Over the past few centuries, our comprehension of the Milky Way has undergone a remarkable transformation. From initial astronomical observations to the advent of advanced telescopes and space missions, we have progressively revealed the intricate intricacies and profound essence of our universe. The Milky Way serves as a captivating laboratory for investigating the evolution of galaxies, offering valuable insights into the life cycles of stars, the creation of stellar clusters, and the dynamics governing astral structures.

Galactic Halo and Dark Matter

Beyond the visible disk of the Milky Way, an extended region called the galactic halo surrounds the galaxy. The galactic halo is believed to contain significant amounts of dark matter. This invisible substance exerts a gravitational influence on visible matter. Understanding the distribution and properties of dark matter within the Milky Way's halo sheds light on the nature of this elusive cosmic component.

As we traverse the Milky Way's cosmic arms, we deepen our appreciation for the sophisticated patterns of galaxies that decorate the universe. Exploring our cosmic residence sparks curiosity about the countless other galaxies that await our discovery. Together, let us continue our cosmic voyage, venturing into the wonders of the universe and expanding our knowledge of the breathtaking galaxies that fill the cosmic ocean.

Different Types of Galaxies and Their Visual Morphology

Within the expansive interstellar collage of the universe, galaxies come in a mesmerizing array of shapes, sizes, and structures. In this section, we will explore the diverse types of galaxies and delve into their visual morphology, uncovering the remarkable variety among these cosmic entities.

Galaxies are classified into different types based on their visual appearance and characteristics. The three main types of galaxies are elliptical, spiral, and irregular, each offering a unique window into the cosmic wonders of the universe.

Elliptical galaxies are characterized by their rounded or elongated shape, resembling an ellipse. They range in size from small to enormous and contain a diverse population of stars. Elliptical galaxies often lack prominent features such as spiral arms, and their stars tend to follow more random and chaotic orbits within the universe. These galaxies exhibit a remarkable diversity in size, shape, and stellar content, offering a captivating glimpse into the vast cosmic landscape.

On the other hand, Spiral galaxies showcase majestic arms that sweep outward from a central bulge. These arms consist of star clusters, interstellar gas, and dust, creating breathtaking cosmic spirals. Spiral galaxies possess a flattened disk-like structure, with their stars and interstellar matter revolving around a central core. The Milky Way, our own stellar home, is a prime example of a spiral galaxy, as are the stunning Whirlpool Galaxy and the iconic Andromeda Galaxy.

Irregular galaxies defy the conventional patterns observed in elliptical and spiral galaxies. They lack a distinct shape or structure, exhibiting a more chaotic and distinctive appearance. Irregular galaxies can arise from gravitational interactions and collisions between galaxies, resulting in their unique and captivating forms. These galaxies often harbor regions of intense star formation and serve as cosmic laboratories for studying stellar birth and evolution.

Beyond these primary categories, transitional forms and peculiar galaxies defy easy classification, further adding to the richness and complexity of astronomic diversity.

The study of celestial morphology provides us with insights into galaxies' formation, evolution, and dynamics. Astronomers unravel the detailed interplay of gravity, gas dynamics, and stellar processes that shape the cosmos by analyzing their shapes, structures, and composition.

As we explore the vast cosmic ocean, we encounter galaxies of all shapes and sizes, each with its unique story and cosmic legacy. The visual morphology of galaxies beckons us to clarify their mysteries, inspiring awe and wonder at the complex beauty of the universe.

Exhilarating Facts About Galaxies and Their Supermassive Black Holes

As we continue our exploration of galaxies, let us now delve into some stunning facts that deepen our appreciation for these cosmic entities and the extraordinary phenomena they harbor.

Did you know the average galaxy is estimated to contain around 100 million stars? Just imagine the sheer magnitude of stellar systems within a single universe, each twinkling light representing a sun-like entity or a fiery celestial giant. These interstellar realms are veritable galaxies within themselves, hosting stellar communities that dazzle the imagination.

However, the size of galaxies spans an astonishing range. From dwarf galaxies containing fewer than a hundred million stars to the largest known super-giants with a mind-boggling one hundred trillion stars, galaxies demonstrate the immense scale of the cosmos. Each star's unique characteristics and place in the cosmic composition contribute to the vibrant symphony of cosmic life.

A significant portion of a typical galaxy's mass, including our own Milky Way, exists in the form of dark matter. Although invisible to our instruments, this mysterious substance exerts a gravitational force that shapes the dynamics and structure of galaxies. The enigma of dark matter intrigues astronomers and fuels ongoing research into understanding its true nature and influence.

One of the most captivating features at the heart of many galaxies is the presence of supermassive black holes. These gravitational monsters, with masses millions or even billions of times that of our Sun, reside in galactic cores. They draw matter into their gravitational embrace, forming accretion disks that generate intense radiation and jets of high-energy particles. Supermassive black holes play a crucial role in regulating the growth and evolution of galaxies, shaping their structures, and influencing the fate of surrounding stars.

We find the supermassive black hole Sagittarius within our Milky Way galaxy. With a mass four million times greater than our Sun, this cosmic titan captivates the imagination, inspiring a deeper understanding of the intricate dynamics and cosmic forces that mold galaxies.

These mind-blowing facts remind us of the cosmic wonders that galaxies hold. From the sheer scale and diversity of stars within a galaxy to the gravitational enchantment of dark matter and the cosmic influence of supermassive black holes, galaxies continue to captivate and challenge our understanding of the universe.

As we venture further into the realms of galaxies, our journey takes us closer to unveiling the elements that shape the cosmos. Together, let us embrace the wonders of galaxies and expand our knowledge of these magnificent cosmic islands that grace the vast expanse of space.

4

Exploring the Universe - From Dwarfs to Supergiants

Description of the Size Range of Galaxies, From Dwarfs to Supergiants

In our journey through the cosmos, we encounter galaxies of all sizes, spanning a vast range that stretches the limits of our imagination. In this section, we will explore the size spectrum of galaxies, from the dwarfs to the colossal supergiants, revealing the extraordinary diversity within space.

Dwarf galaxies, as their name suggests, are relatively small and compact compared to their larger counterparts. These cosmological entities typically contain fewer than a hundred million stars, making them significantly smaller in scale. However, don't let their size deceive you. Dwarf galaxies can exhibit fascinating features and harbor remarkable phenomena, from intense star formation regions to intriguing interactions with neighboring galaxies.

Moving up the size scale, we encounter galaxies of intermediate size, possessing a moderate number of stars and a more substantial cosmic footprint. These galaxies, often referred to as intermediate-sized or medium-sized galaxies, offer a bridge between dwarf and supergiant galaxies. Their properties, structure, and evolution display various characteristics that contribute to the complexity of the stellar landscape.

Supergiant galaxies, on the other hand, are the cosmic Goliath of the universe. These colossal entities boast a mind-boggling number of stars, with estimates reaching a staggering one hundred trillion or more. Each supergiant galaxy is a cosmic metropolis, hosting a bustling population of stars, interstellar gas, and celestial formations on an unprecedented scale. The dynamic interactions and gravitational dances within supergiant galaxies shape their systems, driving the evolution and destiny of their stellar residents.

It is within this vast array of galaxies, from dwarfs to supergiants, that we witness the dynamic and ever-evolving nature of the universe. The size of a galaxy not only influences its individual characteristics but also plays a role in its interactions with neighboring galaxies, shaping the cosmic astral composition we observe.

As we navigate the cosmic ocean, from the compact realms of dwarf galaxies to the expansive realms of supergiant galaxies, we gain a deeper appreciation for the breadth and complexity of the astrophysical landscape. Each universe, regardless of its size, holds within it a treasure trove of cosmic wonders and mysteries waiting to be discovered.

Facts About The Immense Number of Stars in Galaxies

Within the vast expanse of galaxies, an astonishing fact awaits the sheer magnitude of stars that populate these cosmic entities. Let us delve into some mind-boggling facts about the immense number of stars within galaxies, shedding light on the extraordinary cosmic tapestry that spans the universe.

When we contemplate the night sky and witness the glittering stars above, it is hard to fathom the true scale of stellar populations within galaxies. On average, a galaxy contains approximately 100 million stars, each a radiant beacon in the cosmic darkness. Just imagine the sheer magnitude of these stellar systems, illuminating the galactic realms with their brilliance.

However, the number of stars within a galaxy can vary significantly. Dwarf galaxies, although smaller in size, still boast a remarkable number of stars, ranging in the millions or tens of millions. The larger and more massive galaxies, such as supergiants, are home to an awe-inspiring one hundred trillion or more stars, painting a cosmic canvas of epic proportions.

Consider the implications of these numbers. The vastness of the universe, with its billions of galaxies, implies an astronomical number of stars. To comprehend the true scope of this, imagine the grains of sand on Earth's beaches, each representing a single star. Now multiply that by billions upon billions, and you might begin to grasp the vastness of the stellar population inhabiting the cosmos.

These staggering numbers highlight the diversity and abundance of stars that make up galaxies. Each star has unique characteristics, from size and temperature to luminosity and lifespan. The interplay between these stars, their gravitational interactions, and their cosmic journeys shape the evolution and dynamics of galaxies themselves.

The realization that galaxies contain such an immense number of stars invites us to ponder our place in the universe. Amidst this vast cosmic sea, our tiny blue planet is a minuscule speck orbiting an ordinary star within the boundaries of a single galaxy.

As we persist in our voyage amid the celestial marvels of the cosmos, let's appreciate the jaw-dropping magnitude and variety of stars nestled in galaxies. Acting as astral lighthouses, they direct our expedition and fuel our fascination with the riddles concealed in the far reaches. In unison, let's be awestruck by the vastness of the star clusters, setting forth on an interstellar journey that broadens our comprehension of the infinite stars lighting up the expansive canvas of the universe.

The Oldest and Most Distant Galaxy Observed, GN-z11.

In the vast cosmic expanse, as we gaze into the depths of space, our eyes are drawn to a captivating celestial entity: GN-z11, the oldest and most distant galaxy ever observed. In this section, we will embark on a journey to uncover the remarkable story of GN-z11, a window into the early epochs of the universe.

GN-z11 is a testament to the incredible power of astronomical observation and technological advancements. Located at an astonishing comoving distance of 32 billion light-years from Earth, GN-z11 allows us to witness the universe as it existed a mere 400 million years after the Big Bang.

The journey to discover GN-z11 was a challenging feat. It required the combined efforts of cutting-edge telescopes and instruments, including the Hubble Space Telescope and the powerful Keck Observatory. By capturing and analyzing the faintest traces of light emitted by this ancient galaxy, astronomers could discover its secrets and gain insights into the early stages of cosmic evolution. It serves as a cosmic time capsule, preserving a snapshot of the universe's infancy and helping us piece together its narrative.

What makes GN-z11 truly exceptional is its age. As we peer into the depths of space and time, we observe this ancient starlit outpost, a relic from the dawn of the universe. Its existence challenges our understanding of cosmic formation and pushes the boundaries of what we thought was possible.

The discovery of GN-z11 is a testament to humanity's insatiable curiosity and our unyielding quest to discover the perplexities of the cosmos. It invites us to contemplate the vastness of space, the passage of time, and the wondrous events that unfold within its embrace.

As we continue to explore the marvels of the universe, GN-z11 beckons us to push the boundaries of our knowledge, venture further into the cosmic abyss, and continue seeking answers to the fundamental questions that have captivated humanity for centuries.

Together, let us marvel at the astonishing nature of GN-z11, a distant sentinel from the cosmic past. Its discovery opens new frontiers in our understanding of the universe. It reminds us of the boundless wonders that await our exploration.

5

Dark Matter and Cosmic Mysteries

Overview of the Nature of Dark Matter and its Significance in the Universe

Within the profound reaches of the cosmos, concealed from our sight, dwells a perplexing celestial conundrum: dark matter. In this section, we set forth on an expedition to decipher the secrets surrounding dark matter and examine its pivotal part in the genesis, behavior, and transformation of galaxies.

Dark matter, as its name suggests, is a mysterious form of matter that does not interact with light or other forms of electromagnetic radiation. It eludes direct detection, rendering it invisible to our instruments and challenging our understanding of the universe. Yet, its gravitational influence permeates the cosmic landscape, shaping the structures and behaviors of galaxies.

The presence of dark matter within galaxies is inferred through its gravitational effects on visible matter. As astronomers study the motions of stars and gas within galaxies, they notice peculiarities that cannot be explained solely by the visible matter we observe. These anomalies suggest the presence of an additional mass in the form of dark matter.

Dark matter is significant in outer space, providing the gravitational glue that holds galaxies together. Its gravitational pull shapes the distribution of matter within galaxies, influencing the rotation curves of stars and determining the structures of spiral arms. Without dark matter, galaxies as we know them would not exist in their current form.

The exact nature of dark matter remains a mystery, leaving scientists with many unanswered questions. Numerous theories have been proposed, suggesting that dark matter may consist of yet-undiscovered subatomic particles that interact only weakly with ordinary matter. Efforts to detect and understand dark matter are ongoing, pushing the boundaries of scientific knowledge and inspiring new avenues of research.

Dark matter's impact extends beyond individual galaxies. It influences the universe's large-scale structure, contributing to the formation of vast cosmic web-like filaments and clusters of galaxies. These cosmic structures, guided by the gravitational embrace of dark matter, shape the distribution of galaxies on the largest scales.

The study of dark matter not only reveals the aspects of astronomic dynamics but also deepens our understanding of the universe's composition. It prompts us to reconsider the nature of matter itself. It challenges our assumptions about the fundamental building blocks of the cosmos.

As we plunge deeper into the celestial void, let's embrace the riddle that is dark matter, permitting its mystery to spark our inquisitiveness and propel our pursuit of understanding. We will investigate dark matter's part in the astral dance of galaxies, deciphering the concealed secrets within the unseen reaches of the cosmos.

Facts About the Mysteries Surrounding Dark Matter

Fact 1: Invisible and Unseen

Dark matter remains invisible and undetectable through conventional means. Despite its substantial presence in the universe, its elusive nature poses a tremendous challenge for scientists seeking direct detection. Its interactions with ordinary matter are fragile, making it difficult to observe and study in detail.

Fact 2: Cosmic Dominance

Dark matter constitutes a staggering 85% of the total matter in the universe, outweighing ordinary matter by a substantial margin. While stars, galaxies, and planets comprise only a small fraction of the cosmic inventory, dark matter holds sway over the cosmic landscape, shaping its structures and dynamics.

Fact 3: Missing Pieces in the Puzzle

The true nature of dark matter remains unknown, representing one of the most compelling puzzles in modern science. Despite decades of research and numerous experiments, scientists have yet to identify the specific particle or particles that comprise dark matter. Its composition and properties remain shrouded in mystery, leaving much to be explored and understood.

Fact 4: Gravitational Influence

Dark matter's gravitational influence extends far beyond its invisible cloak. It plays a crucial role in the formation and dynamics of galaxies, providing the gravitational scaffolding upon which they assemble and evolve. Without dark matter's gravitational pull, galaxies would not have the stability and coherence required to maintain their structures and preserve their stellar populations.

Fact 5: Cosmic Webs and Filaments

The cosmic web, composed of vast filaments and voids that crisscross the universe, owes its existence to dark matter. This multifaceted cosmic tapestry weaves through space, forming a framework for creating galaxy clusters and superclusters. Dark matter's gravitational influence draws ordinary matter along these cosmic highways, sculpting the vast cosmic landscape we observe.

Fact 6: Dark Matter and the Fate of the Universe

Dark matter's significance extends beyond individual galaxies. Its gravitational effects influence the expansion rate of the universe, playing a role in shaping its ultimate destiny. Understanding dark matter is integral to revealing the intricate interplay between dark energy, dark matter, and ordinary matter, collectively determining the fate of the cosmos.

Fact 7: Inspiring New Theories and Experiments

The intricacies surrounding dark matter inspire scientists to develop innovative theories and experiments. From underground detectors to space-based observatories, researchers strive to unlock the secrets of dark matter. The search for dark matter particles continues, pushing the boundaries of our knowledge and opening new avenues for discovery.

These facts highlight the vastness of the cosmic enigma that is dark matter. As we journey through the universe, let us embrace the challenge of unraveling its mysteries, fueled by the curiosity to comprehend the invisible forces that shape the cosmos. Together, we embark on a cosmic quest, pursuing the answers within the shadows of the universe.

6

Astounding Phenomena in Space

As we voyage through the cosmos, we encounter many extraordinary phenomena that captivate our imagination and challenge our understanding of the universe. In this chapter, we will embark on a breathtaking journey to explore some of the most astounding activities that occur within the vastness of space.

Supernova Explosions

Supernovae, the explosive deaths of massive stars, unleash incredible energy and light into the cosmos. These cataclysmic events mark the end of a stellar life cycle and leave behind remnants such as pulsars and neutron stars. The brilliant display of a supernova explosion illuminates the surrounding space, enriching the cosmos with heavy elements like gold, silver, and uranium, scattering them across space, enriching future generations of stars and planetary systems. The components are forged within the heart of the star.

Gamma-Ray Bursts

Gamma-ray bursts are among the most energetic events known in the universe. These intense bursts of gamma-ray radiation result from the collapse of massive stars or the merger of binary systems, releasing enormous amounts of energy across the electromagnetic spectrum. This burst can last from a fraction of a second to several minutes. Gamma-ray bursts offer a glimpse into the extreme physics of the universe and serve as beacons of cosmic evolution. The energy released during a gamma-ray explosion is mind-boggling, often surpassing the total energy output of billions of stars combined.

Quasars

Quasars, short for "quasi-stellar radio sources," are cosmic powerhouses in distant galaxies' hearts. They are fueled by supermassive black holes devouring surrounding matter, emitting intense radiation across various wavelengths. Quasars serve as cosmic lighthouses, illuminating the early universe and providing insights into galactic evolution and the growth of massive black holes. The light we observe from quasars has traveled billions of light-years to reach us, providing a glimpse into the universe's early stages. Some quasars are so far away that their light reveals the universe as it existed when it was only a fraction of its current age.

Blazars

Blazars are a subcategory of quasars characterized by their intense and variable emission of high-energy gamma rays. They are powered by supermassive black holes with powerful jets of particles pointed directly at Earth. Blazars exhibit extreme brightness and serve as natural laboratories for studying the most energetic processes in the universe. These jets, traveling near the speed of light, produce a range of radiation that includes gamma-rays, X-rays, and radio waves. Blazars exhibit extreme brightness and variability, making them fascinating cosmic objects to study.

Pulsars

Pulsars are rapidly rotating neutron stars emitting radiation beams that sweep across space like cosmic lighthouses, the remnants of massive stars that have undergone supernova explosions. They emit beams of radiation that sweep across space, resulting in regular pulses of emission observed from Earth. Pulsars can rotate hundreds of times per second, and their intense magnetic fields focus and accelerate particles. Their highly regular pulses are scanned across the electromagnetic spectrum, ranging from radio waves to X-rays and gamma rays. Pulsars offer insights into the nature of matter under extreme conditions and provide a unique window into the remnants of stellar explosions. Some pulsars even serve as highly accurate cosmic clocks, rivaling Earth's most precise atomic clocks.

Cosmic Microwave Background Radiation

The cosmic microwave background (CMB) radiation is the faint echo of the universe's early moments, dating back to about 380,000 years, known as the "afterglow" of the Big Bang. It consists of faint microwave radiation that permeates the entire universe. The CMB is often described as the universe's first light, representing the moment photons could finally travel freely through space. It pervades the whole universe, serving as a relic from the hot, dense phase of cosmic infancy. The CMB provides valuable clues about the composition, age, and expansion of the universe, offering a glimpse into our cosmic origins.

These truths augment our admiration for the extraordinary celestial events transpiring within the universe. They serve as reminders of the immense energy, extensive spans, and profound cosmic mechanisms.

7

Unveiling the Local Group: A Galactic Ensemble of Marvels and Interactions

This section will broaden our cosmic perspective beyond the Milky Way and explore the Local Group. This small interstellar neighborhood encompasses our own galaxy and the neighboring Andromeda Galaxy. Join us as we uncover this cosmological ensemble, fascinating details, and remarkable interactions.

The Local Group

The Local Group is a small cluster of galaxies that includes approximately 54 galaxies, gravitationally bound together in a cosmic dance. At the heart of this group lies our very own Milky Way, along with our closest celestial neighbor, the Andromeda Galaxy (M31), and a collection of smaller dwarf galaxies. The Local Group is a testament to the thorough interplay of gravitational forces and cosmic dynamics on a small scale.

The Andromeda Galaxy (M31)

The Andromeda Galaxy, also known as M31, is prominent in the Local Group. Located about 2.537 million light-years from the Milky Way, it is the nearest spiral galaxy to us. With a diameter of approximately 220,000 light-years, the Andromeda Galaxy is slightly larger than the Milky Way and contains a staggering trillion stars. Its majestic spiral arms, dust lanes, and stellar clusters make it a captivating sight in the night sky.

Galactic Collisions

One of the most fascinating aspects of the Local Group is the future cosmic collision between the Milky Way and the Andromeda Galaxy. Due to their gravitational attraction, the two galaxies are on a collision course, culminating in an astronomic merger billions of years from now. This collision will reshape the structure of both galaxies, triggering star formation and leaving a new, combined starlit entity in its wake.

Satellite Galaxies

The Local Group is not solely composed of the Milky Way and the Andromeda Galaxy. It also hosts numerous satellite galaxies, smaller dwarf galaxies that orbit around the more massive galaxies. Examples include the Large and Small Magellanic Clouds, satellite galaxies of the Milky Way, and the Triangulum Galaxy (M33), a companion of the Andromeda Galaxy. These satellite galaxies contribute to the perplexing dynamics and gravitational interactions within the Local Group.

Gravitational Dance

Within the Local Group, the gravitational interactions between galaxies shape their orbits and influence their evolution. Galaxies are not static entities but are constantly in motion and interaction. The delicate balance of gravitational forces determines galaxies' paths, leading to detailed patterns of orbits and alignments within the Local Group.

Exploring the Local Group and the Andromeda Galaxy allows us to broaden our perspective and appreciate the interconnectedness of the cosmic landscape. As we witness the cosmic interactions and foresee the future merger between the Milky Way and Andromeda, we gain insights into our galactic neighborhood's cosmic evolution and dynamic nature.

Together, let us continue our cosmic exploration, embracing the Local Group's wonders and the Andromeda Galaxy's mesmerizing beauty. As we unveil the secrets of this galactic ensemble, we deepen our understanding of the cosmic symphony that unfolds in the vastness of the universe.

Facts About the Vast Cosmic Structures: Sheets, Filaments, and Voids

This section delves into the astral patterns extending far beyond individual galaxies—sheets, filaments, and voids. Brace yourself for mind-blowing facts that shed light on these cosmic landscapes' immense scales and breathtaking beauty.

Cosmic Web

The universe is not a randomly scattered collection of galaxies. Instead, it forms a delicate cosmic web—a vast network of interconnected structures. This web comprises cosmic sheets, filaments, and voids, weaving a mesmerizing tapestry across the cosmos. The cosmic web represents the large-scale distribution of matter, shaped by the gravitational pull of dark matter.

Sheets

Cosmic sheets are immense, flat regions of the universe, stretching across millions of light-years. These expansive sheets are composed of clusters, superclusters, and groups of galaxies meticulously arranged in a filamentary structure. Sheets are like cosmic walls, forming boundaries that define the vast voids between them.

Filaments

Filaments are elongated threads of matter that connect cosmic sheets. They act as bridges, linking galaxies and galaxy clusters. Filaments span hundreds of millions of light-years, elaborately interweaving through the cosmic web. These filamentary structures are rich in matter, forming the backbone of the cosmic web's refined architecture.

Voids

Voids are vast, seemingly empty regions within the cosmic web. These expansive regions stretch between filaments and sheets, creating cosmic voids of unimaginable proportions. Voids can be hundreds of millions of light-years wide, appearing as vast cosmic bubbles. While voids appear empty, they contain traces of matter, including dwarf galaxies, cosmic dust, and sparse gas.

Great Attractor

Within the cosmic web, a gravitational anomaly, the Great Attractor, exerts its pull. The Great Attractor is a region of space that influences the motion of galaxies, causing them to move towards it. This mysterious cosmic structure, hidden behind the Milky Way's center, remains partially obscured. Demystifying the nature and origin of the Great Attractor is a challenge that intrigues scientists.

Revealing the Universe's Grand Design

The study of the cosmic web offers a glimpse into the underlying structure of the universe, revealing the interplay between dark matter, ordinary matter, and cosmic evolution. Through advanced observational techniques and computer simulations, scientists have mapped the detailed patterns of the cosmic web, unmasking the secrets of the universe's large-scale architecture.

Laniakea Supercluster

The Local Group, including the Milky Way and the Andromeda Galaxy, is part of a larger cosmic structure known as the Laniakea Supercluster. Laniakea spans over 500 million light-years and encompasses thousands of galaxies. Within Laniakea, the gravitational interactions of galaxies shape the cosmic flows and guide the motion of astral ensembles.

These facts highlight the awe-inspiring cosmic structures that extend across vast distances. The sheets, filaments, and voids of the cosmic web shape the grand cosmic symphony, influencing galaxies' formation and driving the universe's evolution.

As we contemplate the vastness of the cosmic web, let us be humbled by the puzzling masterpiece that connects galaxies across billions of light-years. The cosmic structures that span the universe remind us of the extraordinary scales at play and inspire us to continue exploring the wonders within the boundless depths of the cosmos.

8

Cosmology - The Study of the Universe

I n this chapter, we embark on a profound exploration of cosmology, the scientific discipline dedicated to understanding the universe. Then, we will delve into the fundamental concepts and captivating discoveries that define cosmology as a branch of astronomy.

Definition of Cosmology

Cosmology is the scientific study of the universe's origin, evolution, structure, and ultimate fate. It seeks to explain the oddities of the cosmos by investigating the fundamental questions about the nature of space, time, matter, and energy on the largest scales. Cosmology combines observations, theoretical models, and mathematical frameworks to deepen our understanding of the universe's grand design.

The Big Bang Theory

At the heart of cosmology lies the Big Bang theory—a widely accepted model that describes the universe's birth. According to this theory, the universe originated from a sweltering and dense state approximately 13.8 billion years ago. The subsequent expansion of space-time gave rise to the universe as we know it today. The Big Bang theory provides a framework for understanding the origin and early evolution of the cosmos.

Cosmic Microwave Background

As mentioned previously, cosmic microwave background (CMB) radiation plays a pivotal role in cosmology. It is the faint radiation left over from the hot, dense phase of the early universe when it transitioned from a plasma to a transparent state. The study of the CMB allows cosmologists to probe the universe's early conditions, test the predictions of the Big Bang theory, and gain insights into the composition and evolution of the universe.

Large-Scale Structure

Cosmologists investigate the universe's large-scale structure, mapping the distribution of galaxies, galaxy clusters, and cosmic voids. By studying these structures, cosmologists gain valuable information about the underlying cosmic web and the processes that shaped the universe over billions of years. Studying large-scale networks provides insights into cosmic expansion, the influence of dark matter and energy, and the formation of cosmic filaments and superclusters.

Dark Matter and Dark Energy

Cosmology also grapples with the mysteries of dark matter and dark energy. Dark matter, which outweighs visible matter in the universe, plays a crucial role in the formation of structures and the gravitational dynamics of galaxies. On the other hand, dark energy is a mysterious force driving the universe's accelerated expansion. Understanding the nature and properties of dark matter and energy are among cosmological research's central pursuits.

Multiverse and Beyond

Cosmology also explores the possibility of a multiverse—an ensemble of multiple universes beyond our observable realm. The concept of a multiverse arises from theoretical models, such as inflationary cosmology, and the search for a deeper understanding of the universe's fundamental laws and parameters. Investigating the concept of a multiverse challenges our notions of reality and pushes the boundaries of cosmological exploration.

Cosmology stands at the forefront of scientific inquiry, striving to uncover the fundamental truths and mysteries that shape our cosmic existence. By peering into the vast depths of space and time, cosmologists provide us with insights into the universe, its origins, its evolution, and its destiny.

Facts about the Big Bang and Cosmic Background Radiation

This section reveals facts illuminating the nature of the Big Bang and the cosmic background radiation. Prepare to be amazed as we explore the remarkable aspects of these fundamental cosmic observations.

The Primordial Fireball

The Big Bang was not an explosion in space but rather the sudden emergence of space and time. In the tiniest fraction of a second, the universe expanded from an incredibly hot and dense singularity, where all matter and energy were compressed into an infinitesimally small point. This primordial fireball marked the beginning of our cosmic journey.

Rapid Expansion

The expansion of the universe during the Big Bang was extraordinarily rapid. In a mere fraction of a second, space expanded exponentially, stretching the fabric of the universe to unimaginable scales. This rapid expansion, known as cosmic inflation, smoothed out irregularities and set the stage for forming galaxies and cosmic structures.

The First Light

As mentioned in the previous chapter, approximately 380,000 years after the Big Bang, the universe had cooled enough for protons and electrons to combine and form neutral atoms. This influential moment, recombination, allowed photons to travel freely through space. These photons, which comprise the cosmic microwave background radiation, carry information about the universe's early conditions and give us a glimpse into its infancy.

The Oldest Light

The cosmic microwave background radiation is often described as the oldest light in the universe. It has traveled through space for over 13 billion years, echoing the universe's early moments. By studying the patterns and fluctuations in the CMB, cosmologists can glean insights into the composition, geometry, and evolution of the universe.

Striking Uniformity

One of the most astonishing facts about cosmic background radiation is its remarkable uniformity. The temperature of the CMB is almost identical in all directions of the sky, with only slight temperature variations of a few parts in a million. This astonishing uniformity challenges our understanding of how such uniformity emerged from the fiery chaos of the early universe.

Nobel Prize Discovery

The discovery of cosmic microwave background radiation is considered one of the greatest achievements in cosmology. In 1964, Arno Penzias and Robert Wilson accidentally stumbled upon the CMB while investigating radio waves. Their groundbreaking discovery earned them the Nobel Prize in Physics in 1978, solidifying the Big Bang theory and paving the way for our understanding of the universe's origins.

The Big Bang and the cosmic background radiation captivate us with their intriguing aspects and offer a glimpse into the earliest moments of cosmic history. They remind us of the incredible journey the universe has taken from a primordial singularity to the vast cosmos we behold today.

As we ponder the significance of the Big Bang and the cosmic background radiation, we are humbled by the intricate cosmic dance that has shaped our existence. Let us continue to unravel the anomalies of the universe, exploring the depths of cosmic time and space and marveling at the astonishing wonders that await our discovery.

9

Astronomy vs. Astrophysics

Differentiating Between Astronomy and Astrophysics

In this chapter, we dive into the fascinating realms of astronomy and astrophysics, exploring these two disciplines' similarities, distinctions, and interconnected nature. Then, we will navigate the celestial landscapes and uncover the nuances that set astronomy and astrophysics apart.

Astronomy

Astronomy is an ancient science that focuses on the observation and study of celestial objects. It encompasses the exploration of planets, moons, stars, galaxies, nebulae, and other cosmic entities. Astronomers use telescopes and other observational tools to collect data about celestial objects' properties, behavior, and interactions. Astronomy is often described as the qualitative study of the universe, seeking to understand its vastness and beauty.

Astrophysics

Astrophysics, on the other hand, is a branch of astronomy that delves into the underlying physics and mathematical principles governing celestial objects' behavior, composition, and evolution. It applies the laws of physics, such as gravity, electromagnetism, and thermodynamics, to study the physical properties and processes occurring in the cosmos. Astrophysicists employ mathematical models, simulations, and advanced instruments to dissect the intricate mechanisms in stars, galaxies, black holes, and other cosmic spectacles. Astrophysics is often considered the quantitative and theoretical counterpart to astronomy.

Interconnectedness

While astronomy and astrophysics are distinct fields, they are intimately connected, with overlapping areas of study. Astronomers and astrophysicists often collaborate and share insights as their research interests and objectives align. Astronomy provides the observational foundation upon which astrophysics builds theoretical models and explanations. Astrophysics, in turn, deepens our understanding of the physical processes underlying the observations made by astronomers. Together, these disciplines contribute to our comprehensive knowledge of the universe.

Historical Perspective

Historically, the boundary between astronomy and astrophysics was less defined. The term "astrophysics" emerged in the late 19th century to denote the physics-based approach to studying celestial phenomena. Before that, "astronomy" and "astrophysics" were often used interchangeably. Over time, as our knowledge of the universe expanded and scientific techniques advanced, the distinction between astronomy and astrophysics became more prominent.

Evolving Fields

Both astronomy and astrophysics are dynamic fields that continuously evolve with technological advancements and scientific understanding. New observational instruments, space missions, and computational tools allow astronomers and astrophysicists to probe deeper into the cosmos, uncovering new developments and addressing previously unanswerable questions. The boundaries between the two disciplines continue to blur as they converge in their pursuit of unraveling the paradoxes of the universe.

Career Paths

Pursuing a career in astronomy or astrophysics can lead to various professional paths. Astronomers often work in observatories, planetariums, or universities, engaging in observational research, public outreach, and teaching. On the other hand, astrophysicists may be found in academic institutions, research facilities, or even interdisciplinary environments, collaborating with physicists, mathematicians, and computer scientists. Both disciplines offer exciting opportunities for those passionate about exploring the cosmos.

Explanation of the Complementary Roles of Observational and Theoretical Astronomy

In this section, we discuss the complementary roles of observational and theoretical astronomy, illuminating how these two approaches work hand in hand to deepen our understanding of the universe.

Observational Astronomy

Observational astronomy focuses on gathering and analyzing data from observations of celestial objects and elements. Astronomers utilize a variety of instruments, such as telescopes, spectrographs, and detectors, to capture light, radio waves, or other forms of electromagnetic radiation emitted by celestial sources. Observational astronomers meticulously analyze these data to uncover patterns, measure properties, and study the behavior of objects across the universe.

Advancements in Observation

Technological advancements have revolutionized observational astronomy, allowing us to probe deeper into the cosmos with increasing precision and sensitivity. Our ability to capture detailed observations has expanded dramatically from ground-based telescopes equipped with adaptive optics to space-based observatories like the Hubble Space Telescope. Observational astronomers study diverse objects, including planets, stars, galaxies, and cosmic anomalies, enabling us to explore the universe across various scales.

Theoretical Astronomy

Theoretical astronomy complements observational astronomy by utilizing mathematical models, simulations, and theoretical frameworks to understand the physical processes occurring in the universe. Theoretical astronomers develop mathematical equations and computational models that describe celestial objects' behavior, formation, and evolution. They use these models to make predictions, test hypotheses, and explain the observational data obtained by astronomers.

Unveiling the Mysteries

Observational astronomy provides empirical evidence and observational constraints that guide the development of theoretical models. Theoretical astronomers, in turn, refine these models to explain the observed events and predict new circumstances that may be discovered through observations. The iterative process between observation and theory drives our understanding of the universe, allowing us to solve its mysteries and push the boundaries of knowledge.

Feedback Loop

The interplay between observation and theory forms a feedback loop that drives scientific progress in astronomy. Observations inspire new theoretical ideas and models, while theories guide the design of observational experiments and the interpretation of data. This feedback loop fosters a deeper understanding of the cosmos, refining our knowledge of celestial objects, their interactions, and the physical laws governing their behavior.

Interdisciplinary Collaborations

The complementary roles of observational and theoretical astronomy often lead to interdisciplinary collaborations. Observational astronomers work closely with theoretical astronomers to refine models, interpret observations, and explore new avenues of research. Additionally, partnerships with physicists, mathematicians, and computer scientists further enhance our understanding of the universe, combining expertise from different disciplines to tackle complex astrophysical problems.

By adopting both observational and theoretical methodologies, astronomers stretch the limits of our understanding, revealing the secrets of the cosmos. The fusion of tangible data and theoretical structures allows us to gain a holistic comprehension of the universe, tracing its journey from inception to its current condition.

10

Amateur Astronomy - Unveiling the Transient

T he Power of Passion

Amateur astronomers are driven by a deep passion for the night sky and a curiosity about the cosmos. With their enthusiasm and dedication, they actively observe and study celestial objects, often pursuing their hobby with advanced equipment and a commitment to expanding their knowledge. This passion fuels their contributions to astronomy and opens new avenues of discovery.

Discovering Transient Events

Transient events are short-lived astronomical events that occur unexpectedly, such as supernovae, comets, meteor showers, and even the occasional outburst of a variable star. Amateur astronomers play a crucial role in discovering and monitoring these transient events. Their vigilance, meticulous observations, and rapid reporting provide valuable data that allows professional astronomers to study these events in real-time and gain deeper insights into their nature and characteristics.

Supernova Discoveries

Amateur astronomers have made significant contributions to supernova discoveries over the years. Their keen eye for detail and commitment to regular sky surveys have led to the detection of numerous supernovae in galaxies near and far. By identifying these stellar explosions, amateurs contribute to our understanding of stellar evolution, galaxies' dynamics, and the universe's distribution of matter.

Comet Hunting

Amateurs have a long and storied history of discovering comets. With their patient sky scans and astute observations, they have been instrumental in spotting comets as they journey through the solar system. These amateur comet hunters contribute to our knowledge of the composition and behavior of these icy visitors, offering valuable insights into the formation and evolution of our planetary system.

Variable Star Observations

Variable stars undergo periodic changes in brightness due to intrinsic properties or external factors. Amateur astronomers play a vital role in monitoring and studying these variable stars. By carefully observing and recording changes in brightness over time, amateurs contribute to understanding stellar pulsations and binary star systems that shape the life cycles of stars.

Citizen Science and Collaborations

The active involvement of amateur astronomers extends beyond individual observations. Many amateurs participate in citizen science projects and collaborate with professional astronomers. These collaborations enable them to contribute to large-scale research initiatives, such as exoplanet discoveries, light curve analysis, and tracking asteroid orbits. The collective efforts of amateurs and professionals enrich our understanding of the universe and foster a sense of community within the astronomical community.

Outreach and Education

Amateur astronomers also play a crucial role in public outreach and education. Their passion and knowledge inspire others to look at the night sky and develop an interest in astronomy. They share their expertise through public star parties, workshops, and online communities, guiding newcomers and kindling a sense of wonder about the universe.

The active role of amateurs in astronomy is a testament to the inclusive and collaborative nature of the field. Their passion, dedication, and contributions make them indispensable partners in pursuing astronomical knowledge. Together, amateurs and professionals push the boundaries of exploration and inspire future generations to gaze at the stars with curiosity and awe.

Next, celebrate the invaluable contributions of amateur astronomers and explore the transient events that shape our understanding of the ever-changing cosmos. Let us revel in their passion, dedication, and unwavering commitment to unraveling the wonders that unfold in the vast expanse of the universe.

Facts About Significant Discoveries Made by Amateur Astronomers

Comet Hale-Bopp

One of the most famous comet discoveries by amateur astronomers is Comet Hale-Bopp. In 1995, Alan Hale and Thomas Bopp independently spotted the comet, marking one of the most extraordinary comets of the 20th century. Their discovery captured the world's attention. Hale-Bopp went on to provide a spectacular show in the night sky for over a year.

Exoplanets

Amateur astronomers have played a pivotal role in discovering exoplanets, planets orbiting stars beyond our solar system. In 1999, amateur astronomer Bill Doyle detected a transit of the exoplanet HD 209458b, becoming the first amateur to observe a planet crossing in front of its parent star. This groundbreaking observation demonstrated the potential of amateurs in contributing to the growing field of exoplanet research.

Supernova SN 2011fe

In 2011, amateur astronomers Pugh and Bode discovered supernova SN 2011fe in the nearby galaxy M101. Their vigilance and sharp-eyed observations enabled scientists to study this particular supernova, contributing to our understanding of stellar explosions and the formation of heavy elements in the universe.

Variable Stars

Amateurs have made numerous discoveries and observations of variable stars, which undergo periodic changes in brightness. One notable example is the amateur astronomer Clyde Tombaugh, who discovered Pluto in 1930 while searching for a hypothetical ninth planet. Tombaugh's discovery forever changed our understanding of the solar system and opened up new avenues of exploration.

Asteroids and Near-Earth Objects

Amateur astronomers have made substantial contributions to discovering and tracking asteroids and near-Earth objects (NEOs). Their vigilant surveys and systematic observations have resulted in the detection of numerous asteroids, some of which have potentially hazardous orbits. These amateur discoveries contribute to our knowledge of the asteroid population and help safeguard our planet.

Lunar Impact Monitoring

Amateurs have actively monitored the Moon for impact events caused by meteoroids striking its surface. Their observations and recordings of impact flashes have contributed valuable data to lunar science, providing insights into the frequency and dynamics of lunar impacts and the potential risks they pose to future lunar missions.

11

Conclusion

As we come to the end of our journey through The Abyss Above: Mind-Blowing Facts About Astronomy, the Cosmos, and Outer Space, let us take a moment to reflect on the fascinating facts and topics we have explored:

We started our exploration by diving into the fundamentals of astronomy, understanding celestial objects, their properties, and the methods used to study them.

We marveled at the immensity of galaxies, learning about their vast numbers, sizes, and the unknowns they hold within.

The enigmatic nature of dark matter captivated our attention as we explored its significance in galaxies and the cosmos.

We delved into the enchantments of the oldest and most distant galaxy observed, GN-z11, and pondered the cosmic origins it represents.

The wonders of space phenomena, from supernovae explosions to cosmic background radiation, left us in awe of the universe's dynamic nature.

Our exploration of the Milky Way and beyond revealed the intricacies of our home galaxy and its place within the larger cosmic landscape.

We marveled at the vast cosmic structures, such as sheets, filaments, and voids, that shape the cosmic web and our understanding of the universe's large-scale structure.

The branch of cosmology offered insights into the origin and evolution of the universe, taking us on a journey from the Big Bang to cosmic background radiation.

We distinguished between astronomy and astrophysics, appreciating their complementary roles in interpreting the cosmos.

The active role of amateur astronomers in unveiling transient events and contributing to discoveries and observations fascinated us, highlighting their passion and dedication.

Final thoughts on the Nature of Astronomy and the Cosmos

Astronomy, the study of the universe, continues to astound us with its profoundness, captivating beauty, and limitless potential for discovery. The cosmos, with its billions of galaxies, trillions of stars, and countless celestial experiences, beckons us to explore its depths and expand our understanding of the vast expanse we reside.

Throughout this book, we have been exposed to the wonders of astronomy, from the grandeur of galaxies to the intricacies of subatomic particles. We have witnessed the power of observation and the role of theoretical frameworks in uncovering the secrets of the universe. We have celebrated the contributions of novice astrologists who, with their passion and dedication, have made significant discoveries and expanded our knowledge of the cosmos.

The inspiring nature of astronomy reminds us of our place in the universe. It ignites a sense of wonder within us. It fuels our curiosity, drives scientific progress, and inspires us to reach for the stars in pursuit of knowledge.

As we conclude this book, let us carry the remarkable facts, insights, and stories we have encountered. Let us gaze up at the night sky with newfound appreciation, knowing that each twinkling star holds a story waiting to be told. And let us continue our exploration of the cosmos, for the universe beckons us to unravel its secrets, one astro nugget at a time.

Epilogue

Encouragement for Further Exploration and Learning in Astronomy

Congratulations! You have completed your journey through The Abyss Above: Mind-Blowing Facts About Astronomy, the Cosmos, and Outer Space. But let this not be the end of your astronomical adventure. Instead, let it be the beginning of a lifelong exploration and a catalyst for further learning and discovery.

The universe is an ever-expanding spectrum of knowledge waiting to be discovered. Countless celestial wonders are yet to be explored, ambiguities waiting to be solved, and new discoveries waiting to be made. So, I encourage you to continue your journey of exploration in astronomy, for it is a field that offers endless opportunities to satisfy your curiosity and expand your horizons.

Take the time to gaze at the night sky and observe the beauty of the stars, planets, and galaxies. Seek opportunities to attend stargazing events, join local astronomy clubs, or participate in citizen science projects. Engage in discussions with fellow enthusiasts, share your observations and insights, and be open to learning from others. Remember, astronomy is a field that thrives on collaboration and knowledge sharing.

Most importantly, never stop asking questions. Let your curiosity guide you on a quest for deeper understanding. Explore the latest research, delve into the scientific literature, and stay informed about new discoveries and advancements. The universe is dynamic, and our comprehension of it continues to evolve. You can stay at the forefront of astronomical knowledge by keeping up with the latest developments.

Additional resources for those interested in delving deeper into the subject

Suppose you're eager to delve deeper into the captivating world of astronomy. In that case, numerous resources are available to aid you on your journey. Here are some additional resources that can help expand your knowledge and satisfy your astronomical curiosity:

1. **Books:**

- "Cosmos" by Carl Sagan
- "A Brief History of Time" by Stephen Hawking
- "The Universe in a Nutshell" by Stephen Hawking
- "The Elegant Universe" by Brian Greene
- "Astrophysics for People in a Hurry" by Neil deGrasse Tyson

2. **Websites and Online Resources:**

- NASA's website (www.nasa.gov): Explore the latest news, images, and discoveries from space missions and research projects.
- The Hubble Space Telescope website (hubblesite.org): Discover breathtaking images and learn about the latest findings from one of the most iconic telescopes in history.
- The European Space Agency's website (www.esa.int): Access information about European space missions, research, and discoveries.

3. **Observatories and Planetariums:**
   Visit local observatories, planetariums, or science centers in your area. Many of them offer public programs, stargazing events, and educational

exhibits.

4. **Online Astronomy Courses and MOOCs:**

Platforms such as Coursera (www.coursera.org) and edX (www.edx.org) offer online courses in astronomy and astrophysics taught by renowned professors from top universities.

Charting the Course: Help Us with Your Review

Thank you for embarking on this cosmic journey through "The Abyss Above: Mind-Blowing Facts About Astronomy, the Cosmos, and Outer Space." We hope you found our exploration awe-inspiring as the vast, starlit expanses we've discovered together.

Your feedback is essential to our mission to share the universe's wonders with other explorers. We invite you to leave a review on Amazon, sharing your thoughts and insights on your journey through the cosmos. Did the book ignite a newfound fascination with the universe? Which facts or sections resonated most with you? Your feedback not only helps us improve but also aids fellow stargazers in choosing their next read.

To leave a review, head to the book's page on Amazon, scroll down to the 'Customer Reviews' section, and click 'Write a customer review.' Your voice can light up the path for others on their journey into the cosmos. Safe travels through the stars.

Resources

American Astronomical Society. (n.d.). https://aas.org/
Astronomy. (n.d.). Caltech Astro Outreach. http://www.astro.caltech.edu/

Astronomy magazine. (2023, July 13). Astronomy Magazine - Interactive Star Charts, planets, meteors, comets, telescopes. Astronomy Magazine. https://www.astronomy.com/

European Space Agency. (n.d.). https://www.esa.int/
Florin Simion Yonescat. (n.d.). Royal Astronomical Society. The Royal Astronomical Society. https://ras.ac.uk/

Hubble Home. (n.d.). Hubble. https://hubblesite.org/
Jenner, N. (2023). 20 amazing facts about space and astronomy. www.sky-atnightmagazine.com. https://www.skyatnightmagazine.com/space-science/facts-about-astronomy-space/

National Aeronautics and Space Administration. (n.d.). NASA. https://www.nasa.gov/
National Air and Space Museum. https://airandspace.si.edu/

SDSS. (2023, June 7). Sloan Digital Sky Survey-V: Pioneering Panoptic Spectroscopy - SDSS-V. SDSS - Mapping the Universe. https://www.sdss.org/

Space.com: NASA, space exploration and astronomy news. (2023, July 16). Space.com. https://www.space.com/

Space News. (n.d.). National Geographic. https://www.nationalgeographic.com/science/space/

Wikipedia contributors. (2023a). Astronomy. Wikipedia. https://en.wikipedia.org/wiki/Astronomy

Wikipedia contributors. (2023). Galaxy. Wikipedia. https://en.wikipedia.org/wiki/Galaxy

www.ingramcontent.com/pod-product-compliance
Lightning Source LLC
Chambersburg PA
CBHW061324120626
46546CB00007B/2671